animal babies
in deserts

KINGFISHER

Kingfisher Publications Plc
New Penderel House
283–288 High Holborn
London WC1V 7HZ
www.kingfisherpub.com

First published by Kingfisher Publications Plc 2006
10 9 8 7 6 5 4 3 2 1
1TR/1105/TWP/SGCH(SGCH)/150STORA/C
Copyright © Kingfisher Publications Plc 2006

A CIP catalogue record for this book
is available from the British Library.

ISBN-13: 978 0 7534 1302 9
ISBN-10: 0 7534 1302 7

Author: Sue Nicholson
Senior Editor: Carron Brown
Designer: Joanne Brown
Proofreader: Sheila Clewley
Picture Research Manager: Cee Weston-Baker
DTP Co-ordinator: Catherine Hibbert
Senior Production Controller: Lindsey Scott

Printed in Singapore

animal babies

in deserts

My short fur is the colour of sand. When I am older, my long tail will be bushy.

Who is my mummy?

My mummy is a dingo and I am her puppy.

It is hot in the desert. We sleep all day and come out at night when it is cooler.

I have a small head and big, beady eyes. My tail helps me to balance when I sit up to look around.

Who is my mummy?

My mummy is a ground squirrel and I am her kitten.

Our stripy, brown fur helps us to hide in our rocky desert home.

I have **hairy ears** and long **eyelashes**. These stop gritty sand blowing in my ears and my eyes.

Who is my mummy?

My mummy is a camel and I am her calf.

When I am bigger, my white fur will turn as brown as my mummy's.

I like to eat seeds. I hold them tightly in my paws and nibble them with my sharp front teeth.

Who is my mummy?

My mummy is a gerbil and I am her baby.

We have long claws on our feet so we can dig tunnels under the ground.

I have soft feathers and a long neck. I look out for danger with my large, black eyes.

Who is my mummy?

My mummy is an ostrich and I am her chick.

We cannot fly, but can run really fast on our long legs.

I have fur in white diamonds around my eyes. My four hooves help me leap across the dry ground.

Who is my mummy?

My **mummy** is an oryx
and I am her **calf**.

When I am older, the
bumps on my head
will grow into **long**
pointed **horns**.

I have creamy yellow fur,
a small pointed nose,
long whiskers and
huge hairy ears.

Who is my mummy?

My mummy is a fennec fox and I am her pup.

My mummy licks my fur to keep me cool and clean.

Additional Information

Deserts are the driest areas on earth and occupy more than one-third of the planet's surface. Many creatures remain hidden throughout the heat of the day and come out only at night when it is cooler. The animals in the book are found in deserts all over the world: dingos live in Australian deserts; Harris' ground squirrels can be found in the Sonoran desert, USA; dromedary camels live in herds in Asia, the Sahara desert in Africa, and in central Australia; gerbils are found in the wild in Mongolia; ostriches and fennec foxes are found in the Sahara desert; and oryxes live in the Kalahari desert, South Africa.

Acknowledgements

The publisher would like to thank the following for permission to reproduce their material. Every care has been taken to trace copyright holders. However, if there have been unintentional omissions or failure to trace copyright holders, we apologize and will, if informed, endeavour to make corrections in any future edition.

Cover: Annebicque Bernard/Corbis Sygma; Half-title: A1Pix/Sunset; Title page: Getty/Gallo Images; Dingo 1: Ardea/Jean Paul Ferrero; Dingo 2: Ardea/Jean Paul Ferrero; Ground squirrel 1: Ardea/Paul van Gaalen; Ground squirrel 2: Getty/Gallo Images; Camel 1: Alamy/Kumar Sriskanden; Camel 2: Frank Lane Picture Agency/Gerry Ellis/Minden Pictures; Gerbil 1: Photolibrary.com; Gerbil 2: A1Pix/Sunset ; Ostrich 1: Corbis Sygma; Ostrich 2: Nature Picture Library/Tony Heald; Oryx 1: Still Pictures/Martin Zwick/WWI; Oryx 2: Nature Picture Library/Tony Heald; Fennec fox 1: A1Pix/Sunset; Fennec fox 2: A1Pix/Sunset